THE BEST BAPTISM EVER

THE BEST BAPTISM EVER

Jenny's Story

by Bette Molgard

Bookcraft
Salt Lake City, Utah

Library of Congress Catalog Card Number: 92-75437
ISBN 0-88494-868-4

Second Printing, 1995

Printed in the United States of America

This book is dedicated to my mother, Barbara Spiekerman, a devoted member of The Church of Jesus Christ of Latter-day Saints. My dad, a wonderful man, was not a member and was active in his church. Mom always took us to church with her. Because of her example her son served a mission, all four of her children were married in the temple, and she has nineteen grandchildren who are all active members of the Church. Thank you, Mom, from all of us and from your future posterity. Because of you, we know that one person can make a difference.

STUCK ON
PLUS FOURS

The timer on the oven buzzed, and I knew I hadn't made it. Mom had said I could try it again, but I was already mad. The thing I don't like the most about second grade is timed tests. Mrs. Barker had told us we needed to write 64 answers in two minutes. Not 63, not 62, but exactly 64 answers to move on to the next timed test. I'd been stuck on plus 4s forever.

My twin brother, Jake, didn't ever have trouble. He was already on plus 9s. And he didn't even try! He never practiced at home. I practiced and practiced and he passed and I didn't. It just wasn't fair!

I can never stay mad at Jake for too long, though. He's so funny, I can't help but laugh at him. He has bright red hair and a million freckles. He can wiggle his ears and cross his eyes at the same time. One night I was grumpy with him, so he hung a spoon on his nose and crossed his eyes at me until I had to laugh.

Mom gave me an understanding look. "It's time to wash up for dinner anyway, Jenny. Maybe we can try again later tonight. Right now, call everyone for dinner."

"Mo—nica! Dad! Jake!" I shouted at the top of my voice. Then I remembered and grinned sheepishly at Mom. "I know, I know," I said in a small voice. "You could have screamed from here yourself."

Mom chuckled, and I knew I wasn't in trouble. I hate being in trouble. It doesn't seem to bother Jake, but it really bothers me.

"Jenny, have you seen Doodles?"

I know it sounds funny, but that's what we call my little sister. She's only one and a half, and she gets in trouble more than all of the rest of us put together. But mostly it's because she doesn't know any better. Her real name is Amy, but the first sound she made was "Dooo, dooo, dooo," so everyone calls her Doodles. And when she wanders off, I usually have to find her. It's kind of exciting, though. You never know where she will be or what she will be doing. "I'll go find her," I volunteered.

I looked in the bedroom—no Doodles. I looked in the family room—no Doodles. Then I heard her in the bathroom. That was not good news. She usually gets in extra trouble in the bathroom, and this time was no different. There she sat, in the middle of a pile of toilet paper. She had emptied the whole roll of it and had it draped over her head and around her neck and was tearing it and throwing it all over. Her squeals and the delighted look on her face told me she was having a great time.

"Doodles," I said, "I think you've done it again. Come on, it's time for dinner."

I untangled her, stood her up, and tried to move her out of the bathroom, but she didn't want to go. She started screaming at the top of her voice and arching her back until I thought that if I held her any longer my arms would break off. But I knew that if I let go, she'd hit her head on the tub. I used to be able to pick her up, but she's too big for me now.

Mom heard the noise and rescued me. "Doodles! That was our very last roll." She picked Doodles up and then turned to me. "Jenny, will you put the toilet paper in a paper bag? We'll just have to take pieces out of the sack until I can go to the store tomorrow."

"Okay." I shook my head and sighed. Somehow, I'd become not only Doodles's seek-and-find sister but her cleanup committee too. If she weren't so cute and funny, I could get mad at her.

We had dinner. I practiced my reading for half an hour, tried my timed test two more times, and gave up. It was time for bed. I thought, "Maybe if I asked Heavenly Father, He would help me with the timed test tomorrow."

Mrs. Barker had said that anyone who wasn't on plus 5s by then would get a *B* on the first report card. I had *A*'s on everything else. I just *had* to pass that test! I said my prayers twice, just to make sure, and went to bed.

THE GREAT DAY

The next morning at breakfast, Mom said I could try my timed test one more time before I went to school. I only had one more practice test, and I brought it to the table so Mom could time me right after I ate.

Doodles sits in her high chair right beside me. She is a really messy eater, so I'm glad she doesn't sit right up to the table. There's always a space in between Doodles and me. I hope there always will be. She gets part of her food in her mouth, part on the floor, and the rest on herself. It's disgusting. Mom always waits until after breakfast to give her a bath. That way, she doesn't need another bath until after lunch.

We were almost through eating when it happened. Doodles sneezed. Little kids don't cover their mouths, they just sneeze. Whoever or whatever is in the line of fire gets plastered. And Doodles sneezed oatmeal all over me—and all over my last practice timed test.

"Doodles! Now I have to change my clothes, and I'll never pass my timed test today!" Doodles threw her spoon at me and laughed. Everyone else laughed too, except me. I ran from the table and cried as I ran up the stairs.

Mom was right behind me. "Jenny, you know Doodles didn't sneeze on purpose. You were so close to passing last night. I'll bet you'll pass it today for sure. Hurry and wash your face with cold water, and change your clothes. I'll pack your lunch." She gave me a hug as I went into my bedroom.

I hoped she was right. But I said my morning prayers twice just to make sure.

It wasn't long before I was in Mrs. Barker's room. Second grade is so much harder than first grade. In first grade, we just had to learn easy stuff, and Miss Leslie gave us hugs and lots of stickers.

I was still scared of Mrs. Barker. She didn't ever hug kids, and her deep voice made me shake. I'd never been in trouble. But Mrs. Barker yelled at almost everyone else, and it made me scared. I got especially scared when she yelled at Jake. He'd already been in trouble three times that morning. He forgot his homework and he kept talking to his friend Danny. Mrs. Barker finally put him at the desk right next to her desk. I've never been put in that desk—I would be so embarrassed if I were, but Jake didn't seem to mind.

I turned to look at him just before the timed tests, and he gave me the thumbs up sign. I knew what he was saying. He was wishing me good luck.

"Jenny, turn around and get your name on your

paper!" Mrs. Barker's voice boomed at me, and I jumped. My heart was already going five hundred miles an hour because of the test, and she'd made it go even faster. I quickly wrote my name on the back of my paper, said a fast prayer (Mom told me that I could pray anywhere), and waited for the starting signal.

"Ready," said Mrs. Barker. I moved to the front of my chair. "Go!"

I wrote as fast as I could, my tongue going as fast as my pencil. My whole body was shaking. I remembered not to erase, just to cross out the mistakes. I went as fast as I could—and just as Mrs. Barker said, "Stop!" I finished. I couldn't believe it. I had finished! Sixty-four problems, and I had done them all in two minutes!

I stood with my hands on my head waiting for Mrs. Barker to call for plus fours. We always have to stand up like that as soon as she says stop. Then we wait for her to call our timed test number. She says she wants to make sure no one cheats and writes down more answers after two minutes. I don't think anyone would dare cheat in front of Mrs. Barker. But this time none of that mattered. I had passed!

Mrs. Barker had us play the quiet game while she corrected our tests. I didn't care if I got a turn to stand up and choose someone else who was being quiet. I just wanted to see a star on the top of my paper. Only two people had finished the test in time, so she had to correct just two papers. What was taking her so long? The suspense was killing me!

Finally, Mrs. Barker announced that Danny had missed two, so he hadn't passed. Then she said what I had been waiting for. I *had* passed plus 4s. I couldn't wait to get home. Mom would be so proud!

I don't remember much about the rest of the day.
Mrs. Barker gave me some plus 5s to practice, and I
finally got to go home.

A HARD DECISION

The minute I opened the door, I started shouting. "Guess what, Mom! I passed plus 4s! I prayed, and Heavenly Father helped me pass it. I knew He would help me!"

"Oh, Jenny, I'm so proud of you, Mom said. "I knew you could do it!" Doodles caught on to the excitement and clapped her hands as she jumped up and down. I gave her a hug, then went upstairs to my bedroom. I sat on my bed and looked at the big red star on the top of the test paper. I was so happy.

Then I saw something that made me feel sick inside. Right in the middle of the paper was 7 + 4 = 12. How could that be? Mrs. Barker corrected it and she had said I hadn't missed any. But I knew that 7 + 4 = 11. I had answered it right three other times on the test, so that meant I knew the answer, didn't it? I wrinkled the test up so no one could see it, and threw it in the garbage.

Mom called me at dinnertime and told me to bring my paper so Dad could see what I'd done in school. I didn't know what to do. I guessed I'd figure it out when I got downstairs.

"Jenny, let's see that timed test. I understand that you finally passed plus 4s. Way to go!" Dad was excited, but it wasn't so much fun as it had been when Mom was excited.

"Oh, Dad, I forgot to bring it down. I'll show it to you after supper." I thought maybe, if I was lucky, he would forget about the paper after dinner. But my stomach always hurts when I tell a lie. It had been such a good day. What was I going to do?

"How did your plus 9s go today, Jake?" asked Dad.

"I finished 62, so the next time I'm sure I'll get 64. They're easy—as long as you know the nine trick. The answer is always one less than the other number, and you stick a one in front of that number. So 7 + 9 = 16, because 6 is one less than 7. Jenny was the only one who passed a test today. Now she has an *A* too."

I should have felt happy. Nobody knew but me. But all I could think about was that wrong answer. Sixty-three problems right, and one wrong. That wrong problem had ruined my day. And I had thought Heavenly Father had helped me.

Later that night, I was still feeling awful. I decided to talk to Mom about it. Some things just didn't make sense to me.

"Mom . . . doesn't Heavenly Father always answer prayers?"

9

"Of course He does, Jenny. We're His children, and He loves us. He helped you pass your test today, didn't He?"

"Yes . . . but what if I hadn't passed it? Would that mean that He hadn't answered my prayers?" I asked.

"Of course not. Heavenly Father always answers prayers, but sometimes He says no and sometimes He tells us we need to wait. He knows us, and He knows that sometimes we learn more if He doesn't give us exactly what we ask for when we ask for it."

That made sense to me. Maybe Heavenly Father wanted to teach me something. I knew what I had to do, but it wasn't going to be easy.

A GOOD LESSON

The next day I was tired first thing in the morning. I hadn't slept much. I just kept thinking about my test and my report card, Mrs. Barker and my family. I thought maybe my family would be disappointed because I would get a *B*, but I knew I wouldn't feel right with an *A* that I hadn't earned.

But every time I thought about talking to Mrs. Barker I kind of panicked. What if she got mad at me? What if she yelled at me? I was so scared, I didn't eat much breakfast.

"Jenny, are you feeling all right?" asked Mom.

"My tummy hurts a little, but I'll be okay," I said.

"She's probably lovesick," teased Jake. "I saw her playing kissing tag with Tyson."

"I was not," I shot back. "He was chasing me, and I was just trying to get away."

"Yea, sure," said Jake.

11

Sometimes he makes me so mad. But my mad feelings only stayed with me a few minutes and then my scared feelings returned. I sure needed some good luck—soon!

That was it!

"Monica," I asked my older sister, "remember that necklace you wore for the band competition?"

"You mean my lucky charm necklace?" she asked.

"Yes. Do you think I could wear it just for today?"

"You want to wear my silver necklace? You're just in second grade. How do I know you wouldn't lose it?"

"I wouldn't lose it, I promise . . . pleeease?" I was half scared of Monica too. She's fourteen, and she gets mad really easily, but I was desperate for extra help.

"All right. But if you lose it, you're really going to get it," she threatened.

"I won't lose it. I promise. Thank you!" We ran upstairs together. Sometimes it was great having an older sister, even though she was a grouch most of the time.

I left for school early. I had smoothed out the test as much as I could. I knew Mrs. Barker would be in her classroom. No students were allowed in the room before eight-fifteen, so I made sure I would be there by eight-ten. I hurried out of the house quickly so Jake wouldn't be able to go with me. I wanted to be alone with Mrs. Barker.

I had to use the side door to the school because our outside door was still locked. It seemed a long way up the hall to her room.

She was sitting at her desk when I walked in. "Jenny, you know you're not supposed to come in for another five minutes. Now you turn right around and march yourself back down that hall and out the door!"

Her words made my knees shake so hard I didn't think I could have marched. I stood there and stammered, "Mrs. Barker, I didn't really pass the timed test yesterday. I thought you might like to know before you did the report cards."

"What do you mean you didn't pass it? I corrected it myself and put the star on the top." She sounded mad, just as I'd feared.

But I went on. "I know you did, Mrs. Barker, but when I got home, I saw that I had missed one. See, look at it."

She took the paper from my shaking hand. "Well, I'll be. . . . Do you know what this means, Jenny?" she asked. Her voice was softer than before.

"Yes," I said, and I could feel my bottom lip start to shake. "It means that I'm still on plus 4s and that I will get a *B* on my report card." I sniffed and wiped my eyes as I looked down at my timed test on Mrs. Barker's desk.

"Jenny, look at me. I'll let you have another chance at an *A* on your report card this morning because you were honest. If you pass it, you'll still be on plus 5s today at school. But the fact that you told me about it means something else. It means that Jenny Jacobs can be trusted. And that's much more important to me than knowing that you know the answer to 7 + 4."

That awful feeling inside of me was gone. There was a warm feeling that spread from somewhere around my heart to my whole body. I guess it showed on my face, because Mrs. Barker gave me a hug. (I hadn't thought that would ever happen, and I wondered if she wanted me to keep it a secret, but I didn't ask.)

"Are you ready to try your test right now, Jenny?" she asked.

"I guess so," I said, and my heart started beating hard again. I touched Monica's necklace once for good luck and said a fast silent prayer: "Please, Heavenly Father, let me pass it!"

And I did pass it. All sixty-four problems. (And I double-checked three times.) And this time, there was a great feeling. I wanted to tell the world, but nobody knew I hadn't passed it the first time.

I even knew why I hadn't passed the first time. I was never going to forget how miserable a wrong decision had made me feel and how good a right decision felt. I'll bet Mom was right. Heavenly Father knew I needed to learn about those feelings.

WHERE'S MONICA'S NECKLACE?

Even the rest of the school day went well for me. But Jake talked to Danny once during class—just once—and it turned out to be one too many times for Mrs. Barker. She didn't put him in the trouble desk. She moved him forever, so that Jake and Danny sat all the way across the room from each other. I thought that was a great idea.

After the move, Jake sat right beside Dumbo. I know that isn't his real name. His real name is El-wood J. Blackendorf, and he's the new kid in school this year. I'd really have to think for a long time if I were given the choice between Dumbo and Elwood. But all the kids in my class and most of the other kids at school call him Dumbo. That's not very nice, but his ears are really, really big. They stick out farther than anybody else's ears I've ever seen. Anyway, nobody wanted to be his friend. But he's the one Jake sat by. He surely wouldn't get in trouble for talking in class anymore.

To top off my extra-good school day, my first-grade teacher, Miss Leslie, had outside recess duty. We ran over to get a hug from her and said, "Guess what, Miss Leslie?"

"What, Jenny?" she asked.

"Jake and I are going to be eight next week, and we get a birthday party. Then the next Saturday we're going to get baptized!"

"That's a lot going on in the next couple of weeks!" exclaimed Miss Leslie.

Just then the bell rang, and we lined up by the door.

It was time for math again. Another timed test—and I hadn't even practiced last night. Oh, well. I was wearing Monica's good-luck necklace. I reached up to touch it for one more bit of good luck—but it was gone! I thought I'd had it when I was outside for recess. I knew my life was over. Monica had said she would kill me if I lost it. I knew she wouldn't really kill me, but I always wish I weren't around when she gets mad. In fact, she's right up there on the same list Mrs. Barker is on, the list of people I don't want mad at me ever.

By the end of the timed test (I only got to the second line) I was so upset that I could feel a big, awful lump in my throat. What if I didn't find Monica's necklace? What if someone else found it and took it home? I tried not to cry, but some tears squeezed out. Finally my friend Jamie went up to tell Mrs. Barker that something was wrong with me. Mrs. Barker called me up to her desk.

"Jenny, are you upset because you didn't get very far on the timed test?"

I looked at my feet and said a quiet no.

"Then what is the matter?"

"I think I lost my sister's necklace out on the playground at recess." By the end of the sentence, I was really crying. I didn't want to cry, and I didn't mean to, but I couldn't help it. I was really going to be in trouble.

"Jenny, why don't you take Jamie outside with you and see if you can find it?"

I let out a big sigh and thanked Mrs. Barker. Jamie and I went out and looked all over the playground. We found a quarter and a hair ribbon and even a shoe. (How could anyone go in from recess and not know that he'd lost a shoe?)

I was ready to give up, and I could feel that big lump coming to my throat again. Then Jamie suggested that maybe someone had put it in the lost-and-found already. There were two lost-and-found closets. One was on the side of the school for the older kids, and we checked there first. The other one was on our side. Monica's necklace wasn't in either closet.

We walked back, and I sat down at my desk. "Did you find the necklace, Jenny?" Mrs. Barker asked.

I just shook my head to say no. The lump made it so I couldn't say anything else.

It was time for art. We were coloring a color wheel. We learned that the primary colors are red, yellow, and blue. I already knew that from a song we learned in Primary at church. Then Mrs. Barker took pieces of red, yellow, and blue chalk and mixed them together. The red with blue on top made purple. The yellow with red on top made orange. And the blue with yellow on top made green.

She told us those were secondary colors. She gave us a piece of paper with circles and squares and told us to make a color wheel like the one she had on the board, except that we were supposed to use our crayons—just our red, yellow and blue—to make all the primary and secondary colors.

When I opened my box of crayons, I remembered that I had let Jake use my red crayon the last time we'd had art. He'd lost at least half of his crayons already since school started. I walked over to his desk and whispered to him that I needed to use my red crayon and that he could use it when I was done. That's when I saw Monica's necklace in the tray of Dumbo's desk!

"Elwood! You have my necklace in your desk!"

He looked surprised. "What do you mean?"

"Give me back my necklace!" I was louder than I meant to be, and Mrs. Barker came to see what was going on.

"Elwood, do you have Jenny's necklace?" she asked.

"No. . . . I mean—it was in my desk, but I didn't take it."

"Then how did it get into your desk? Did it walk there from outside?" Mrs. Barker was mad. And I was glad she was mad. She should've been mad. Dumbo had taken Monica's necklace, and now he was lying about it.

"Elwood, we have talked and talked about what to do if you find something out on the playground. You know the rule is to ask in your classroom and then to take it to the lost-and-found. You will stay in for recess for a week and write, 'I will not keep things that do not belong to me,' on a paper as many times as you can write it during those recesses."

Now Dumbo was crying, and it served him right. And it didn't make any difference to anyone else that he couldn't go out to recess. Nobody played with him anyway.

And I was happy. I had Monica's necklace back, and I was going to give it to her the minute I got home.

JAKE TALKS

It had been a long day, and I decided to read on my bed after dinner. Jake came in and told me he needed to talk to me. I knew it must be important if he was in the house. It wasn't even dark yet. He was always outside playing until Mom made him come in. I moved over on the bed until he could sit down.

He looked to make sure no one was in the hall, and started talking very quietly. It was kind of scary—but kind of exciting.

"Jenny," he said, "Elwood didn't take your necklace. I don't know who did, but it wasn't him. I think someone put it in his desk just to get him in trouble."

"How do you know that?" I asked.

"Because I was with him all recess."

"Well then, why didn't you tell Mrs. Barker that when she got mad at him?" I asked him, but I thought I already knew the answer. I would have been afraid to say anything to Mrs. Barker when she was mad like that. But Jake had a much better reason.

"Because I was afraid we were all going to be in trouble if I said anything."

"Why?" He just wasn't making a lot of sense.

"Because"—he lowered his voice—"Danny had brought some matches to school. His dad smokes, and he just took some of his dad's matches. Elwood was with us. He's not so bad, Jenny."

I looked at him as if he were just a little crazy, but he continued: "Elwood, Danny, and I were trying to set some of the leaves on fire that are over by the fence. We kind of sat close together so no one could see what we were doing."

"What! Jake, you were playing with matches? You could have gotten burned!" I was being louder than Jake wanted me to be, and he quickly shut the door.

"Shshshsh! Jenny, I promise—I'll never play with matches again. It was scary. We just barely got the leaves burning a little bit and Elwood saw a third-grade kid coming over."

"What did you do?" I couldn't believe Jake would play with matches. Well, maybe I could. Jake was always in trouble for something.

He continued. "I didn't know what to do. The fire was just little, but if that kid told on us, we would've all three been sent to the principal's office. But Elwood saved us."

"He did? How?" Somehow I couldn't picture Dumbo being a hero.

Jake smiled. "He sat on the fire and put it out."

"He *what?*" I started to laugh. I couldn't help it. I could just picture Dumbo sitting on the fire. Pretty soon we were both laughing so hard we almost fell off the bed.

When I settled down, though, I started to think about what could happen to someone who sat on a fire. "Jake," I said, "didn't he burn himself?"

"No, he had been sitting on the grass when he was helping to light the fire. Remember, they had just watered the lawn before recess. So he kind of sizzled when he sat down." We both got the giggles again.

"But if Dumbo was with you, how did Monica's necklace get in his desk?" I asked.

"I don't know. You know how everyone is mean to him. Even I used to be mean to him. But now that I have to sit by him, I've started talking to him, and I kind of like him."

I laughed a little to myself. That was just like Jake. It really didn't matter which person poor Mrs. Barker sat Jake by. He could talk to anybody—even Dumbo.

He continued, "I think someone was just trying to get him in trouble. If Elwood had wanted to keep that necklace, it wouldn't have been right in the front of his desk. He would have hidden it."

We talked some more. Jake decided that he would tell Mrs. Barker in the morning that Dumbo had been with him all recess. We decided that she didn't need to know what they'd been doing. We just didn't want Dumbo in trouble for something he hadn't done.

BUT WHO'S GOING TO BAPTIZE US?

The next morning, Mom reminded us that we needed to choose who was to baptize us in a couple of weeks.

Mom is a Mormon, but Dad isn't. I don't want you to think I don't have a good dad, though. He's a real good dad. He takes us fishing and camping. He always reads us a story at night. Then he rocks us to sleep. I know that sounds funny, but it's a game that Jake and I have played with him every night since we were little.

I always have the first turn. He rocks me in the big rocking chair, and I pretend to go to sleep. Then he always tells Mom, "Oh, dear! Jenny has fallen fast asleep. I guess I'll have to carry her up to bed." I try not to laugh, but I usually can't help smiling. Then he carries me up to bed, lays me down, and pulls the covers up while I still pretend I'm sound asleep. He kisses me good night and tries to sneak out the door. I always say, "Good night, Daddy," and he laughs a little and says, "Good night, Princess." I love it when he calls me Princess.

Then he goes back downstairs and rocks Jake to sleep. Jake always starts to snore *loud*, and Dad says, "I think this one has fallen asleep too. I'd better take him to bed." And he walks up the stairs with Jake snoring like a pig all the way. I laugh when they go past my room. It sounds so funny.

Most people at church think that just because Dad doesn't go to our church, he's different. But he's not. He's a good dad. But he couldn't baptize us.

I asked Monica who had baptized her.

"Grandpa Tolson did," she said. "It was so neat. I remember how I felt when I came out of the water. And then on Sunday, he confirmed me."

"But Grandpa Tolson is in the spirit world. He can't baptize me. Who else could baptize Jake and me, Mom?" I asked.

Mom thought for a minute, then she said, "Well, there's Uncle John or Bishop Lee—or Brother Henderson."

Hmmm . . . That was a lot to think over. I knew I would never choose Brother Henderson. He's our home teacher. He comes in every month and shakes Mom's hand and says, "Good evening, Sister Jacobs," and then he shakes Dad's hand and says, "Good evening, Brother Jacobs." Dad hates to be called Brother Jacobs. He's even said that to Mom. But he's always nice to Brother Henderson.

After shaking hands, Brother Henderson sits down and asks us how we all are. Then he doesn't know what to say next, so there's always a big quiet time until Mom thinks of something. Then another long quiet time until Mom thinks of something else to say. I'm always glad when he leaves.

Bishop Lee is nice, but I didn't know him very well because he'd only been our bishop for three months. I was scared to go in for my interview with him so he could tell if I was worthy to be baptized. When I told Mom I was scared, she said that was silly and that I shouldn't be scared because the bishop is Trisha's dad.

That's true. The bishop is Trisha's dad. But I'd never been in a room alone with anyone's dad but my own. I'd be glad when my interview was over.

Jake decided to ask Uncle John. He's funny and always tells jokes and even likes to play kickball and Frisbee with us. He has hair the same color as Jake's, and he even has freckles. I wanted to ask Uncle John, too.

But then I started thinking about Uncle Jerry. He's Mom's other brother.

He just started going to church last year. Before that, Mom said he wasn't living the way Heavenly Father wanted him to live. Then he was in a motorcycle accident. He's in a wheelchair now, but he's doing a lot of things right. I couldn't really figure how he could baptize me, but if he could, I wanted him to.

"Mom," I asked, "Has Uncle Jerry ever baptized anybody?"

Mom thought for a minute. "Well, he was just made an elder, so he has the power to baptize and confirm. But I don't think many people would think of him. In fact, I'm not sure how he could baptize you. But I could call him and ask, if you're sure you want me to."

I was sure. I would be the first person Uncle Jerry baptized. That would be an extra special baptism. This was really going to be exciting!

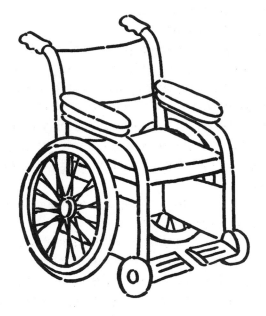

THE INTERVIEW

I sat on the padded bench outside the bishop's office with Mom and Doodles. Jake was in talking to the bishop. Bishop Lee had told us that he would take the oldest one in first. Ever since I could remember, Jake had told everyone we met for the first time that he is my "older" brother. He was born two whole minutes before I was. I had always wished that I had been first so that I could be Jake's older sister. But tonight I was relieved to be the second one born. It meant that I could be the second one to go into the interview. I was scared to death!

I was worried that I wouldn't be able to answer the questions. I thought it was going to be something like a test. I was afraid that I might flunk it, and then I'd never get to be baptized. Jake is so smart, he'd pass for sure, and his dumb twin would be the only person that anyone knew who had flunked the bishop's interview. That would be so embarrassing!

The door opened, and my heart started trying to pound out of my chest. My mouth was dry, and when I stood up my knees were shaking. The bishop stepped into the hallway with his arm around Jake's shoulders. "You have a great son here, Sister Jacobs. He's ready for baptism, and we'll be proud to have him as a baptized member of our ward. Jenny, are you ready for your interview?"

I smiled and said a quiet yes, as if I really felt ready. Right then, I would rather have been anywhere but heading into the bishop's office.

He closed the door and asked me to sit down in the big wooden chair in front of his desk.

"I always thought it would be fun to be a twin. You and Jake will always have someone special to be part of your life. That's great." He smiled at me, and I smiled back and nodded.

"Well, let's get right into the interview. Jenny, why do you want to be baptized?"

I thought for a minute. Baptism is something that you always know is going to happen when you're eight because that's the age Heavenly Father knows you can be counted on to make the right decision. But I knew why I wanted to be baptized. "I want to be a member of the Church."

"I'm sure you do. It is a very special church. It's the only church that has the authority to baptize. It's Jesus' true church, and if we want to be members of His church, we need to be baptized."

I must have given the right answer. Maybe I could pass the interview. But then he asked me a really hard question.

"Jenny, do you know what a covenant is?"

I didn't know the answer, and I wanted to cry. I guess the bishop could see that, because he stopped for a minute and explained some things to me.

"It's all right if you don't know all the answers, Jenny. This is a special time when I can talk about how important baptism is and talk about the promises that are made at the time of baptism. I know that your Primary teachers and your Mom have taught you everything that we're going to talk about. But the baptism interview is one of my favorite things I get to do as a bishop.

Now, if you don't know what a covenant is, I'll just tell you. A covenant is a very special promise that you make with Heavenly Father and that He makes with you."

I knew about the promises. I just didn't know that they were called a covenant. I breathed a sigh of relief. This wasn't going to be so hard as I had thought it would be.

"I know the promises that I will make," I said. "I promise to follow Jesus and to do what He would want me to do."

Bishop Lee smiled, and I started to relax. "That's exactly right, Jenny. And if you will always remember Jesus, and try to keep His commandments, then you have kept your part of the covenant. Do you know what Heavenly Father promises you?"

"I'm not sure."

"Then I'll remind you. (He was still smiling, so I knew it was all right.) Heavenly Father promises that He will forgive you when you make mistakes, if you will repent. Do you know what repentance is?"

"My Primary teacher says it's like a big eraser. When we have done something that we shouldn't do, we pray to Heavenly Father and ask Him to forgive us, and promise to try to never do it again. Then that mistake is erased."

The bishop liked that idea. He nodded his head and said that I was exactly right. Then he said that Heavenly Father has two more promises. He promises that He will give us the help of the Holy Ghost to make decisions, and that He will give us eternal life with Him if we live worthily.

The bishop was right. There was nothing in the interview that was new to me. We had talked about things that I had been taught ever since I could remember.

He filled out a paper and gave it to me as he stood up. "Jenny, I believe you're ready to be baptized."

He shook my hand, and I knew the interview was over. It hadn't been a test at all. It had been a nice talk. And now Jake and I really were ready to be baptized. I could hardly wait!

THE BIRTHDAY PARTY

We never go to school on Wednesday afternoons. We call it *half-day* because we go to only half a day of school. The other half of the day, the teachers fix lessons to teach us for another week. We love Wednesdays.

One Wednesday was even better than usual. Jake and I were going to have our birthday party. Mom had let us invite four friends each. She said that ten second graders would be plenty for a party. I knew it would be a great party. We were planning to go to the swimming pool and then home, where a clown was going to show us some tricks. After that, we would have ice cream and cake and open our presents.

The only bad part about the party was that Jake had invited Dumbo. He could have invited anyone, but he chose to invite Dumbo. I couldn't believe it. I didn't want Dumbo at my party, but I didn't get a choice.

Our friends all came with their towels and swimming suits. We had to stay in the shallow end. Mom was going to watch from the bleachers and hold Doodles.

Jake had brought a penny. He'd throw it in the water, and he and his four friends would dive for it. At least, he and three of his friends would dive for it. Dumbo kept getting water in his nose. He would come to the surface and sneeze while the other boys went down to get the penny.

We girls laughed at Dumbo and watched the boys for a while. Then we decided that we would have a tea party. We would all hold our breath, sit on the bottom of the pool, and pretend that we were sitting at a table. One of us would pour from a pretend pitcher, and the rest of us would hold out our pretend cups and drink from them. That all had to be done fast because we couldn't hold our breath for very long. But it was fun looking under the water at my bubbly friends. They looked all blurry under water with their cheeks all puffed up and their eyes all big trying to hold their breath.

We got to swim for only an hour, so it wasn't long until it was time to go.

Bongo the clown was there when we got home. She had a huge orange bunch of hair, and green and white clown clothes. Her shoes went way out from her feet—almost two feet long—and they flopped and flipped as she walked. She pulled quarters out of all our ears and gave them to us. Then she changed her quarter into a dime and then into a penny. We couldn't figure out how she was doing it.

When it was time for us to blow out the candles on our cake, Bongo said that she had some special candles for Jake's cake. Everyone sang happy birthday to me, and I made a wish and blew out all my candles.

Then we all sang "Happy Birthday" to Jake, and he made a wish and blew. The candles looked as if they were going to go out. In fact, they did go out—and then they lit up again.

Jake got the funniest look on his face, and blew them out the second time. And they came back on again! We were all laughing and laughing. His face looked so funny, and he was laughing and blowing so hard that his freckles were disappearing into his red face.

Finally, Jake said, "Bongo, what are these candles made out of?"

Bongo was laughing so hard that her makeup was running in streaks down her face. "They're trick candles, Jake. No one can blow them out. They just keep staying on and staying on. You've been such a good sport that I'm going to check your head for extra money."

Jake grinned. "Check my head for what?"

"Extra money. People have to be extra smart to be good sports. And you laughed right along with us. You must have some extra money in your head."

Bongo told Jake to stand up. She lifted up a small bucket and tipped Jake's head so that his ear was inside of it. Then she told him to shake his leg. He did, and quarters fell out of his ear into the bucket! There was a whole pile of them. The whole thing looked and sounded so funny that we all started laughing again. Jake's eyes were huge, and he felt in his ear to see if there was any more money. I guess Bongo had cleaned him out, because there was nothing left in his ear.

Then Bongo blew a balloon up for each of us and made it into an animal. I got a long pink dog, and Jake got a blue giraffe. Bongo was done. She waved good-bye to us all and flip-flopped out of the door. We were sorry to see her go, but we knew that it was time to open our presents.

I opened mine first. I got some Barbie doll clothes, a T-shirt, a box of sixty-four crayons with a sharpener in it, and some bows for my hair.

It was Jake's turn. He got some matchbox cars, a bubble-gum machine, a hundred-piece puzzle, and a pencil. Yes, a pencil—the kind you get out of the pencil machine at school that cost fifteen cents. That's what Dumbo brought.

Jake was nice about it. He said, "Hey, a Rams pencil! I don't have a Rams pencil in my football team collection. It's great, Woody. Thanks!"

Jake had decided that he wasn't going to call El-wood by that name anymore. But he had said that "Woody" was a good nickname. He wanted us all to call Dumbo "Woody."

I didn't know what to call him. All I knew was that I didn't like him.

Mom drove all of our friends home, and that was the end of our birthday party. It had been fun. And I crossed out another day on my calendar. Only three more days until we were going to get baptized! I could hardly wait!

THE BIG DAY

Uncle Jerry had told Mom that if I wanted him to baptize me, he would figure out a way to do it.

The morning of my baptism, Mom told me to get my special baptism book and write down the date. I tried to use my best handwriting as I wrote "Saturday, November 2" on my baptism page. I won't learn how to write in cursive until next year, so I used my best printing. I don't think I will ever forget that day—no matter how old I am.

Uncle Jerry was to pick me up at 9:30. He had told me to wear my swimming suit. It's a good thing that it was still hot outside, or Mom wouldn't have let me go. Uncle Jerry'd said we had a lot to do to get ready. Jake and I were going to be baptized at 11:30, so whatever Uncle Jerry wanted had to be done in a hurry. Mom had told him to have me home by ten-thirty.

He drove up in his van and honked. I love to ride in his new van. At first Mom was nervous, because Uncle Jerry drives using hand controls. He has hand brakes and can make the van go fast and slow by using just his hands. He has to use his hands because his legs don't work at all.

I jumped in the van, and we drove to the car wash. Uncle Jerry said that the only way he could baptize me would be to have someone carry him and his chair into the baptismal font. And if his chair was going to be in the font, it had to be really clean.

Uncle Jerry opened the door of the van and pushed some buttons, and the little elevator on his van lifted him down to the ground. Then he handed me some money and I put it in the slot. Uncle Jerry and I hosed off his wheelchair—and ourselves. It was so funny. The water kept splashing on us as it hit the spokes and seat of his wheelchair. It's a good thing that we had our swimming suits on. We were soaked!

Then we got back into the van. I went home to take my shower, and Uncle Jerry went to his house to get ready.

At eleven-fifteen we were at the church. I was so nervous! I asked Jake if he was nervous, but he said I was silly. He and Uncle John had practiced in another room just a few minutes before, so he knew what to do. Uncle Jerry wasn't at the church yet. It takes him longer to get ready than it does people with legs that work. I hoped Uncle Jerry and I could practice before the meeting started.

We all went into the Primary room. It was pretty nearly filled up. Jake and I had our bishop, our Primary president, our Aunt Jody, our Grandma Tolson, Mom, Dad, Doodles, Monica, and the uncles who were going to baptize us—and Dumbo and his mom. Jake had invited them.

Uncle Jerry didn't get there in time to practice. I hoped he knew how to do it. I didn't.

Jake and Uncle John went first. Uncle John raised his hand, called Jake by name, and said, "Having been commissioned of Jesus Christ, I baptize you in the name of the Father, and of the Son, and of the Holy Ghost. Amen." Then Jake squeezed his nose and went under the water. That is, most of him went under the water. The bishop said his toe had come up, so Uncle John said everything over and put Jake under again. That time, he went all the way down under the water. His hair is extra red when it's wet. When he came up, I noticed his red hair first, and his grin that spread from ear to ear second.

Then it was my turn. Mom took me into the dressing room and held the door open that led to the font. Uncle John and another dad that was dressed in white were lowering Uncle Jerry and his chair into the font. He held his hand out to me and I went down the steps. Uncle Jerry winked at me as he took my hand, and I knew everything was going to be all right.

He placed my hands in the right position, said the same words that Uncle John had, leaned way over in his wheelchair and baptized me. I had to go under only once!

I had felt the warm water on the outside of me as I went down into the water. But I had the neatest feeling when I came out. I felt warm all over inside. It was a wonderful feeling, and I knew that Jesus and Heavenly Father were happy that day because I was a member of The Church of Jesus Christ of Latter-day Saints.

THE VERY GOOD, VERY BAD SUNDAY

The next day was Sunday. It was fast Sunday. In our family, we don't fast until we're eight years old and have been baptized. That Sunday was not only the day I was going to be confirmed, it was also the first day I was fasting. I was really hungry, but Mom said that we could eat when we got home.

After the prayer, the bishop said it was time to confirm Jake and me. He said we were going to go in alphabetical order. We had learned about *A-B-C* order in school this year. The *a* in Jake came before the *e* in Jenny, so Jake would be first.

That was fine with me. I wanted to watch and see how Jake did everything. I didn't want to make a mistake in front of everyone.

Jake went up and sat on a chair. Uncle Jerry, Uncle John, Brother Henderson, and the bishopric put their hands on his head. I wondered if the hands felt heavy.

Uncle John spoke. He told Jake to receive the Holy Ghost, and then gave him a blessing. Then Jake shook hands with everyone who had been in his circle and sat down.

Then it was my turn. Uncle Jerry confirmed me. When he said, "we say unto you, receive the Holy Ghost," that warm feeling was all over me again. It felt nice, and I wanted to stay feeling that way forever.

When Uncle Jerry passed me the sacrament, I didn't take the bread. I just passed it on. After all, I was fasting, and I knew bread was food, so I shouldn't be eating it. I wasn't going to be tricked into breaking my first fast.

Uncle Jerry looked at me funny and then leaned over and asked me why I hadn't taken the bread.

I told him I was fasting.

He whispered that the sacrament was different from other food. He said that the sacrament wouldn't break my fast. So I quickly whispered to Jake to pass the bread back to me.

After I put the bread in my mouth, I opened the zipper on the case of the scriptures that Grandma Tolson had given me for my baptism. (My scripture case was blue and Jake's was black so we wouldn't get them mixed up.) I had put in the side pocket the picture of Jesus that the Primary president had given us during our interview for baptism. She had said that we should take the picture out during the sacrament and think about Jesus. She'd told us we should try to remember what Jesus would do when we have decisions to make.

I tried to think what it would have been like if I had been a little girl when Jesus was on the earth. I looked at the little girl in the picture. She was sitting on Jesus' lap. I decided to pretend that I was the little girl in the picture. I smiled just thinking about it.

When sacrament meeting was over, Jake and I walked to the back of the chapel on the way to Primary. There, sitting on the back bench, were Dumbo and his mom. They were at our church again. And Dumbo wasn't even dressed in his Sunday clothes. He was in his old Levi's from school, with an old school T-shirt. They were the same clothes he had worn for the baptism. I couldn't believe his mom would let him wear that outfit twice into a church. It wasn't nice enough to wear to church.

But then I noticed his mom's dress. It wasn't very nice either.

Jake didn't seem to notice Dumbo's clothes. He told Dumbo that he hadn't seen him during sacrament meeting and was glad that he had come.

Mrs. Blackendorf asked if we were going home right then.

Jake told her that the kids would go to Primary. He asked if Woody could go with us.

I hoped she would say he couldn't. I didn't want to have anyone see that Dumbo had come to our church to see Jake and me confirmed. I didn't want them to see that Jake was friends with Dumbo. They might think that Jake was like Dumbo. And because Jake and I are twins, they might think that *I* was like Dumbo.

But Mrs. Blackendorf said that she would be happy to have Elwood stay with us. Jake told her that the big people stay in the chapel for Sunday

School, and she said that she would like to stay too. I rolled my eyes. Then Dumbo, Jake, and I went to Primary.

When it came time to sing the "Hello" song to the visitors, Jake took Dumbo up in front of everyone. The boys in the Blazers class behind me laughed and whispered. I knew what they were saying. They were making fun of Dumbo's ears and his clothes. I was so embarrassed that I wanted to crawl under my chair. Why did Jake have to be everyone's friend? This very, very good Sunday had turned into a very bad day, and my warm, wonderful feeling was gone.

POOF!

It was three-thirty on Monday afternoon. I had been the first one to come home from school and was trying to finish reading my book so I could write my book report. Mrs. Barker makes us write a book report every month. It can't be on an easy book. The book has to have at least fifty pages. I'm not a fast reader like Jake. He can read a book and write a report during the first week of the month. Mom says I'll be a great visiting teacher—I get mine done during the last week of the month, just in time.

When I first walked in from school, I knew something was going to happen. None of Doodles's toys were in the front room, and everything was clean. I don't want you to think that we live in a dirty house. We just live in a house that looks as if we live in it, and it looks as if Doodles especially lives in it. But it didn't look like that that afternoon.

When Mom told me that the missionaries were coming, I understood.

They'd never come to our house before. Brother Hartman had asked if we could give them dinner Monday night, and Mom had told him that as long as they didn't try to get Dad to come to church they could come. I also knew that meant we were going to have a wonderful dinner. We always have extra-good dinners when we have company.

Mom was busy in the kitchen. I could hear pots and pans and silverware clanging and banging. I could tell she was in a hurry. She wanted everything to be just right by five o'clock.

It was quiet in our house that afternoon. Jake and Monica weren't home from school yet, and Doodles was still having her afternoon nap.

Then Mom came running out of the kitchen, untying her apron as she ran. "Jenny," she told me, "Doodles is asleep, and I have just run out of flour. I thought I'd have enough to make the apple dumpling dessert we like to have with ice cream, but my can is empty. Would you listen for Doodles while I run to the store?"

I told her I could do that, and she ran out to the car as fast as she could go. I wasn't worried. She would just be gone about fifteen minutes, and Doodles would probably stay asleep.

But a couple of minutes later I smelled a new smell. Mom's dinner wasn't the only smell in our house anymore. It smelled good, but I couldn't figure out what it smelled like for a minute. Then it dawned on me. It was baby powder, and the smell was coming from upstairs.

I ran up faster than Mom had gone to the car. When I got to Doodles's room, I knew that I had come at least two minutes too late. Doodles, who had just learned how to get out of her crib, had climbed out and found the big can of baby powder that Mom had left on the bookshelf. She was covered with white, and so was her red carpet. And she was having a great time poofing that powder all over the place.

When I yelled, "Doodles!" she jumped, then looked up and grinned at me. She said something I couldn't understand. But when I tried to take the baby powder away from her, she said her favorite words: "No! No! No!"

The more I tried, the more the baby powder poofed. By the time I had finally got it away from Doodles, we both had baby powder all over us. We smelled good, but we looked as if we were ready to be ghosts for Halloween.

"Doodles," I said, "stop crying. We need to get this cleaned up. The missionaries are coming for dinner. Come and help me get the vacuum cleaner out of the closet."

She was still sniffing a bit, but she followed me to the closet and helped me pull the vacuum cleaner out. At least she thought she was helping me. It would have been easier to do it by myself.

We pulled the vacuum cleaner into the bedroom, and I plugged it in. I thought the vacuum cleaner would suck all the baby powder up and that would solve the problem. But it didn't. The vacuum cleaner started to poof the baby powder. It made billowy clouds as it sucked some powder and poofed some powder. Doodles thought it was great. She laughed and pounded the bed where she could see more baby powder. There we were—with Doodles poofing, the vacuum cleaner poofing, and me trying to take care of the whole mess, when Mom came into the room. I thought she'd be mad, but she started laughing at us. I guess we did look funny, both of us busy in our cloud of baby powder. Pretty soon we were all laughing—until Mom saw what time it was.

She ran to finish making dinner and called over her shoulder to clean up Doodles and just shut the door. She said that we could clean it up later. She didn't think the missionaries would want to look in Doodles's room anyway.

I was busy and Mom was busy until everyone was home. The missionaries arrived right at five.

We all sat around the table. Mom had asked Dad to carry the piano bench in for Jake and me to sit on. That left our two extra chairs for the missionaries. Mom made sure that they weren't sitting anywhere close to Doodles. She didn't want Doodles sneezing on their suits.

One was a wide, short missionary and the other a tall, thin missionary. They looked kind of funny together. Their names were Elder Johnson and Elder Monson. We laughed when they told us their names. They told us to call them the rhyming missionaries.

They didn't talk about the Church, just as they had promised they wouldn't, but they did tell us about where they lived before their mission. Elder Johnson was from Minnesota, and Dad said that his grandfather had helped to settle Fergus Falls, Minnesota. Elder Johnson said he lived close to Fergus Falls, and they visited for a long time about Minnesota.

Just before they left, the missionaries said that Mrs. Blackendorf had asked them to come to teach her and Elwood the missionary lessons. They knew that Elwood was our friend, so they thought we would be interested. Jake was excited, but I wasn't. I didn't say anything, though. I just made a face at Doodles, and she laughed.

Then Elder Monson said he had a niece that was Doodles's age when he left on his mission. That changed the subject, and we didn't talk about Dumbo anymore. I was glad. I didn't know why, but I always had a bad feeling when we talked about Dumbo or when I was around him.

When the missionaries were finished eating, they thanked Mom and Dad for the dinner and left.

I had to finish my book report, so Monica helped Mom clean the kitchen. I went to my bedroom and stayed there until Dad was ready to rock us to sleep.

CHAPTER

AN UNEXPECTED HERO

The day started out to be normal enough. We had breakfast, and Jake said he was going to go over to Woody's house after school.

I asked him why he was hanging around Dumbo so much. I didn't mean to say "Dumbo" out loud. I usually only think bad things about him. I never say things out loud.

Mom's eyebrows went down as she turned around and asked, "Jenny, what did you call him?"

"I called him Dumbo—but I didn't mean to. He is weird, though, Mom. He doesn't wear nice clothes, and his ears are big, and, well, I wish he wouldn't come to our church anymore."

I knew as soon as I was finished that I had said more than I should have said. But this Dumbo thing was making me mad. My life had been a lot better without Dumbo always hanging around my twin brother.

"Jenny," Mom said quietly, "do you have any idea why Elwood doesn't wear nice clothes?"

"No." My voice was even softer.

"Elwood's dad died of cancer last year. They didn't have any insurance, and they still have doctor bills and hospital bills to pay. They live in an old trailer down by the railroad tracks because they can't afford to live anywhere else. Before Elwood's dad got sick, they lived in a nice home across town and had nice clothes. Then they had to move into the trailer, and into our school area."

Then she looked at me and asked, "You haven't been mean to him at school, have you?"

"No . . . I promise . . . but I haven't been very nice to him either. I don't feel good around him."

"Jenny," Mom said, "could it be because you think mean things about him? You know that the Holy Ghost doesn't help you to feel good when you're not doing the right thing. Jesus says that we need to love everyone."

"Love! Mom, I can't love Elwood!"

Mom smiled and then said, "There are a lot of ways to love people. Do you love me the same way as you love Jake?"

"No."

"Do you love Daddy the same way as you love Monica?"

"No."

"Do you love Doodles the same way as you love your first-grade teacher, Miss Leslie?"

"No."

"Jesus says to love everyone, but sometimes that means just to remember that everyone is a child of

God. Because you know that, you need to be nice to everyone."

I had never thought of that. I knew why I hadn't felt good around Elwood. I had felt so good when I had been given the gift of the Holy Ghost, and then I had shooed the Holy Ghost away with my mean thoughts. I wasn't going to do that anymore. I was going to remember that Dumbo—I mean Woody—is a child of God, just like me.

I told Mom what I had decided. She gave me a hug and my lunch money, and Jake and I left to go to school.

The rest of the day was a regular day, except that I played with Jake and Woody during recess. I couldn't believe that I had been so wrong about Woody. He really was fun to play with.

Before recess was over, I told Jake and Woody that I would walk them to Woody's trailer after school and then go home. It was a little out of my way, but I didn't have anything better to do.

We were on the way to Woody's trailer when it happened. I still can't believe it. We were walking along and talking. We got to a corner, and I sat down on the curb to tie my shoes. Jake and Woody started to cross the street. They had just gone a few steps when I heard the brakes of a car squeal as it tried to stop. I looked up to see Woody push Jake out of the way, and Woody get hit by the car. He hit the bumper of the car, went up on the hood, and then fell onto the road. He didn't move after he fell.

I ran over to Woody, and so did Jake. Then we heard the car squeal again. That time it was the tires squealing. The man driving the car raced around us and didn't even stop to help. I knew he thought he was in trouble, but when he left we were all alone.

49

Woody was lying so still that Jake and I thought he was dead. There was a bad cut on his forehead, and it was really bleeding. His eyes were closed, and he wasn't even moaning.

I didn't know what to do. Jake said he would get some help, and he ran up the steps and onto the porch of the house on the corner. He started banging on the door. All I could think to do was to pray. So I sat right beside Woody and closed my eyes and said, "Heavenly Father . . . Please don't let Woody die. He saved Jake. And I'm scared and don't know what to do. Please let Jake find someone to help us."

I didn't say "Amen." I just kept praying. I know it wasn't very long, but it seemed like forever before another car came down the street. I squinted in the sunlight reflecting off the car, and thought I recognized the car. When the driver got out of the car, I started crying. It was Bishop Lee's wife, and she grabbed a blanket from the back seat and ran over to help me.

At the same time, Jake came out of the house with a lady who was walking with a cane. He said that he had called 911, and that an ambulance was on the way.

Just about the time that we heard the ambulance siren, Woody opened his eyes. Sister Lee told him he needed to lie really still and quiet. She had covered him up with a blanket, and had put her hand right over the cut on his head. She was pushing hard on his forehead and had stopped the bleeding.

It wasn't really cold outside, but Woody was shaking.

The ambulance people brought a board with straps on it out of the ambulance. They asked

Woody where he was hurting. He said he hurt everywhere, but that his leg was really hurting.

They replaced Sister Lee's hand with a white piece of material, and she stood up to let the ambulance workers talk to Woody. She put one arm around Jake and one arm around me. I was glad Sister Lee had been the person in the car.

The ambulance workers were careful with Woody's leg, and they rolled him onto his side and put the board right up behind him. Then they rolled him onto his back so that the board was underneath him. They buckled the straps around him, picked him up, and put him into the ambulance.

The police came just before the ambulance left. They asked Sister Lee to tell them what had happened. She told them that she hadn't seen what had happened—that we were the only ones who had seen Woody get hit. They took our names and address and said they would come to our home when our parents were there.

Sister Lee told them she would get Woody's mother and take her to the hospital. We got into her car, and she took us home. She waited in the car until we made sure that Mom was home, and then she went to get Mrs. Blackendorf.

The minute we came in, Mom could tell something was wrong. When she asked us, both Jake and I started talking, trying to tell Mom everything at once. Mom couldn't understand anything, so she told us both to stop and take a big breath. Then she asked me to tell her what had happened.

I started to tell her, but when I got to the part about Woody saving Jake, I started crying so hard that Jake had to finish.

When he got through, Mom hugged us both and asked if we would like her to say a prayer with us. We knelt down by the couch right then to thank Heavenly Father for protecting Jake. And then we asked Heavenly Father to watch over Woody at the hospital. It's a good thing Mom was the one to give the prayer. Jake and I were both crying.

CHAPTER

FASTING FOR
A REASON

We didn't hear anything from the hospital that night. But two policemen came to our house after Dad got home from work. They wanted to know if we remembered anything about the car or the man in the car. They said it was against the law to leave after you hurt someone. I thought that was a good law. The man had hurt Woody with the car, and then he had hurt us by leaving us alone when Woody was hurt.

All Jake could remember was that the car was green. He had seen it only from the front and only for a second.

But I told them I had been sitting on the curb, and that I had seen the whole car from the side. They asked if I remembered what shade of green it was.

I told them it was the color of the green peas you get out of a can. I also remembered that it was a station wagon like Sister Lee's, except that it was older and uglier. I told them I thought the man didn't take very good care of his car because one of the windows on the side was just a piece of plastic taped over the window with silver tape.

One of the policemen said he had seen a car like that parked at the house next door to Simon's Market. They said they would let us know if they found out anything.

Dad rocked us to sleep that night. At least I pretended to fall asleep. But when I got in bed I was wide awake. I kept thinking about Woody and talking to Heavenly Father. The last time I looked at the clock, it was nine-fifty-five.

When Mom woke me up in the morning, she said she would call Sister Lee before we left for school to find out if she knew anything about Woody. Mom thought Woody's mom would probably have stayed at the hospital all night. There wasn't a phone at Woody's house, anyway.

When Sister Lee answered, she said she had stayed with Mrs. Blackendorf until late the night before. She said the bishop and his counselor had gone to see Woody and had told him about priesthood blessings. Woody had asked if he could have one. They had given him a blessing, and he was soon fast asleep.

The doctors were going to do tests that morning to see what kind of damage had been done. They knew he had a broken leg, and they had stitched up his head. They needed to check to see if anything inside was hurt.

Sister Lee said their family was going to fast for

Woody that day and asked if we wanted to join them.

When Mom hung up, she told us what Sister Lee had said. Jake and I asked why fasting would help.

She explained to us that when we have an extra special reason that we want a prayer answered, we can fast. She said fasting is like an extra line put into our call for Heavenly Father's help. He knows how much we want that prayer answered when we add fasting to our prayers.

Jake and I both asked if we could fast. We knew it would be hard at school, but we really wanted to help Woody. Monica said she would fast and Mom was going to fast. It felt good to have so many extra lines into Heavenly Father. We were glad we hadn't eaten breakfast yet that morning.

It really wasn't hard to fast through school that day. It was different from the first day we had fasted on the day we were confirmed. That Sunday, all I had been able to think about was how hungry I was. At school this day, all I could think about was Woody.

At lunchtime, Mrs. Barker was on outside lunch duty. Jake and I were the first ones outside, because we weren't eating. Mrs. Barker was sitting on the grass, so we sat down beside her. She asked us how we had gotten finished eating so quickly.

I wasn't really afraid of her much anymore and Jake never had been afraid, so we told her all about Woody. We told her about the accident and how he saved Jake. And we told her that we were fasting.

Then I told her about Woody's problems before the accident. I told her about his dad and their bills and their trailer. I told her I wished there was something we could do to help. She thought a minute and then said she would tell Mr. Woodward. He was in charge of the student council. She thought they might come up with something that would help.

That afternoon, in the middle of science, Mrs. Blackendorf came into our class. She looked tired, but she was smiling. She told Mrs. Barker that she had come to get some homework for Elwood. She had just brought him home from the hospital. She said he had a broken leg, and that the cast went from his toes to above his knee. He would be in a wheelchair for a while, but other than the broken leg and the stitches in his head, he was fine. And he would be back to school on Monday!

Jake and I were so happy we were ready to burst. I knew that Heavenly Father had answered our fasting and prayers. Woody was going to be just fine! I said a quick prayer at my desk. I didn't even close my eyes, but I wanted Heavenly Father to know that I knew who had helped Woody.

A WONDERFUL
ASSEMBLY

We visited Woody several times before Monday. He was lying on his couch on a blanket every time we were there. He had a little TV to watch and a tray to eat on.

Mom had taken us to the store. We had bought him a coloring book and some crayons and some comic books. He was really excited to get our presents. He said it was really boring on the couch.

Monday morning, Jake and I waited outside the school for Mrs. Blackendorf to bring Woody. When she arrived, she took a wheelchair out of the trunk of the car and we helped get Woody out of his side of the car into the wheelchair. Mrs. Blackendorf was in her Sunday dress, and she said she was going to stay for an assembly. She said she didn't know what the assembly was about, but that the principal had stopped by her home and invited her to be there.

At nine o'clock we all went into the assembly. We have all of our assemblies in the gym. We don't have a stage. We leave our chairs in our rooms and sit on the floor Indian-style. That way we can see people who are standing up.

The two policemen that had come to our house were on chairs in front of the gym with Mrs. Blackendorf, Mr. Woodward, and the student council. I was awfully curious by the time the student body president asked us to be quiet.

We all said the Pledge of Allegiance, and then Mr. Woodward asked Jake and Woody to come up to the front. As Jake was pushing Woody's wheelchair to the front, Mr. Woodward handed the microphone to one of the policemen.

The policeman waited until Jake and Woody were beside him. Then he said: "Last week, Elwood Blackendorf and his friend Jake Jacobs were walking home from school. A car driven by a man who had been drinking came down the street heading right for Jake and Elwood. Elwood didn't even think about what might happen to him. He only thought about his friend Jake. He pushed Jake out of the way, and Jake didn't get hit by the car. But Elwood got hit, and you can see by his stitches and his cast that he got hurt pretty badly.

"Elwood had time to get himself out of danger, but he chose instead to get his friend out of danger. For that reason, we would like to give Elwood a special award.

"Every year, our city gives awards to citizens who we think have been heroes. We give these awards out as soon as we hear about what they have done and then we honor them at a banquet at the end of the year. This year, we are proud to include Elwood

Blackendorf as one of the city's 'Heroes of the Year.' His picture and a plaque will be in the City Hall building in a trophy case reserved for all the heroes we have honored. We will also award another plaque to Elwood so that he can always remember the day he chose to save his friend rather than himself. You should be proud that you know Elwood Blackendorf, one of our city's Heroes of the Year."

He handed Elwood a wooden plaque that was gold on the front and had some writing on it. As he did, the sixth-grade students and all the teachers stood up and clapped. And pretty soon everyone was standing and clapping. It wasn't a little clap like we give when we want to be polite. It was a great big sound. Everyone was clapping for Elwood. And Elwood sat in his wheelchair with a red face and a great big grin. Mr. Roberts from the newspaper was there to take pictures, and he took a picture of Elwood and Jake next to each other when everyone was clapping.

Then Mr. Woodward thanked the policemen for coming and said the student council had an idea. He told us that the student body president, Jaren Thomas, would tell us about it.

Jaren told us about how much it costs to go to the hospital. He said that the student council didn't think that a hero's family should have to pay hospital bills. So they had decided that starting one week from that day, we should try to bring all our pennies and nickels to school. He said that the student council would bring around a sheet and we would all throw in the pennies and nickels we'd brought. Then Tuesday we should bring our dimes. Wednesday we should bring our quarters, and Thursday we should bring any money we wanted to give. Then we would have another assembly the next Monday and give the money to Mrs. Blackendorf to help pay for the hospital bills.

Everyone thought it was a great idea. Mrs. Barker had said she thought the student council could come up with a good idea, and she was right.

Then the student council said they had a song they wanted to sing for Elwood. They sang, "Did You Ever Know That You're My Hero?" I don't know if that's the name of the song, but those are the important words. They must have practiced for a long time, because they sounded really good. I got goose bumps all over my arms and legs. My mom gets goose bumps when she's really happy, and I guess I must take after my mom.

Then I looked over in the corner of the gym, and there was my mom. She didn't just have goose bumps. She was crying. I guess she was thinking about what could have happened if Woody hadn't pushed Jake out of the way.

When the assembly was over, we all went back to our classes. Mrs. Barker told us that maybe we could ask our neighbors for their extra change. And maybe our moms and dads could ask people at work. We'd have to wait for a week, but I had a feeling that the sheet was going to be really heavy.

A DAY IN COURT

Ever since the accident, I'd thought a lot about the man who hit Woody with the car. I thought so much about him that I started having nightmares about him. In the nightmare, he would drive up in his green car to the corner where I would be standing, and turn his head and stare at me. His eyes were buggy, and he had eyebrows that were black and bushy and always slanted down to the middle. His teeth were big and crooked and yellow. And he always had on a half of a smile, as if he wasn't even sorry that he'd hurt Woody.

I really had no idea what the man looked like. But that must have been how I imagined he would look, because I kept dreaming about him.

I told Jake about my dreams. He said that since the man in the green car was such a scary guy, we should call him the Boogie Man.

Mom had gone up to talk to the policemen after the assembly. The one who gave Woody his plaque had said that the man was drunk when he hit Woody with his car. She asked the officer what else he knew.

The policeman said that the day after we had told him about the pea green car, he and another officer went to the house next door to Simon's Market. The car wasn't there, but a man answered the door. He was drunk, and yelled at them, "You already picked me up yesterday. Get off of my property and leave me alone!"

The policemen left and went back to the police station to check with the other officers and see who had picked up the man the day before.

Officer Dale had stopped the car. He said that at three-forty-five he'd spotted the car driving fast and not very straight. He had pulled the car over, and could tell that the man had been drinking. Officer Dale said that he had taken him down to the police station and made him blow into a machine that showed he'd had way too many drinks to be driving on the road.

He said he had driven the man home and kept his car. The man was going to go to court the next week.

When the two officers put their stories together, they knew they were talking about the same man. It was the man that had hit Woody with a car and had driven away fast. School had let out at three-thirty. Mrs. Barker never lets us leave the room until we "vacuum" it with our hands. Every paper needs to be picked up before we leave. We had left the class-room five minutes late that day. The man must have hit Woody with the car, driven away fast, and been picked up by the other policeman right afterwards.

The policemen told Mom that someone would be contacting us. They wanted us to go to court and tell what we knew about the accident.

Mom told us everything she knew. When she said we had to go to court, I panicked. I didn't want to meet the Boogie Man. He was too creepy—and I hated him for what he had done to us. I knew that I could never forgive him.

The next day we found out we had to go to court on that Friday. I worried about meeting the Boogie Man all week. Friday morning we got dressed in our Sunday clothes and headed for court. We picked up Woody and his mom on the way. Woody was still in his wheelchair, so Mom had to help get him into the car and then fold up the wheelchair and put it into the trunk.

I looked around when we got into the court room. No one looked like the Boogie Man, so I knew he wasn't there yet.

There were other people I didn't know. There was a man in the front sitting with another man. A lady in a green dress sat behind him with two big boys who looked as if they were in high school.

Everyone had to stand up when the judge came in. Then the judge sat down and so did we. He looked at some papers and then asked one of the men on the front row some questions.

Mom leaned over and whispered that the man that just spoke was the man who was driving the car. I couldn't believe it. I said, "He couldn't be the one. He looks normal." He didn't look at all like the Boogie Man of my dreams.

Mom smiled and put her arm around me.

There was a lot of talking that I didn't understand or even listen to very much. I had always thought that mean men looked mean. How could this man be my Boogie Man?

When the man got through speaking, we took turns telling what we remembered. First Jake spoke, then Woody, and then it was my turn. The man who asked me the questions was really nice, so it wasn't so scary as I'd thought it was going to be. I got a good look at the man I had called the Boogie Man and still didn't believe a man that looked like that could be so mean.

Finally, the judge decided what would happen to the man. It sounded as if he were speaking a language from another country. I didn't understand any of it. When he was done, Mom said court was over.

We all stood up again when the judge left. Then the lady behind the man put her hand on his shoulder. Mom said, "That must be his wife and children. They have really been through a lot of pain, too."

All of a sudden, the Boogie Man came towards us, holding his wife's hand. His head was down and he was looking at the floor, but he was walking right toward us. I leaned closer to Mom.

"I know this won't help much, but I want you to know that I am so sorry for the pain I have caused you. When I drink, I don't think right . . ." and the Boogie Man started to cry. "I would never hurt anyone on purpose, or leave two little kids by themselves to look after someone I had hurt. I'm just not like that."

He looked up at Mom and Mrs. Blackendorf. Tears were rolling down his cheeks. "I hope you can find it in your hearts someday to forgive me."

He looked at Mrs. Blackendorf. "I'm glad that the judge said that the money I will pay to the court for my fine will be given to you to help pay for your son's hospital bill."

Mom said something about wishing him luck on getting his alcoholism under control. They talked for a few more minutes and he and his wife and boys left the courtroom.

"Mom," I asked, "what is alcoholism?"

"Jenny," she explained, "do you remember what the Word of Wisdom says about not drinking any strong drink?"

"Yes. You're not supposed to."

"Well, Heavenly Father knew it would be harmful to our bodies. Alcohol is a drug. And some people who take one drink want another drink and then another. Their bodies just keep telling them to get another drink and another and another. They use up all their money, lose their jobs, and cause a lot of trouble for their families. They find themselves doing things because of the alcohol that they normally wouldn't do. The alcohol makes it so that they really can't think right."

"You mean," I asked, "that man might really be a nice man if he weren't drinking so much?"

"That's exactly right, Jenny. Alcohol is a horrible drug. If that man had never taken a drink, he probably would have been able to stop before he hit Woody. And even if he couldn't, he wouldn't have left you alone to take care of Woody."

That was a lot for me to think about. I had gone into the courtroom hating the Boogie Man. Now I just felt sorry for a man who had made a mistake. I felt sad for him, and I felt sad for his wife and his boys.

But I knew that Heavenly Father had a repentance eraser for that man just as He has an eraser for me when I make mistakes. I wished everything would work out for the man and his family, and I felt better inside than when I had hated the Boogie Man.

REAL HAPPINESS

The fund raising idea was exciting to watch. Every day, four of the student body officers would come into our classroom holding a sheet at each of its four corners. They had already been to the kindergarten rooms and the first grade rooms. They would go in order until they were finished walking through the rooms of all six grades of our school.

The first day it looked as if all the kids had cleared out their piggy banks. The sheet was already sagging when they came to our classroom. We threw our pennies and nickels into the sheet. Jake and I had been around our block, and all the neighbors seemed to be happy to give us all of their change when we told them what we were going to use it for.

Some of our class had butter bowls full of pennies; some, plastic bags. Jake and I had a canful.

Mrs. Barker had a huge bottle. It took her a while to dump all the pennies out of it. She said she had been saving them for twenty years and that she couldn't think of a better way to spend them.

The student body officers told our class that when they got finished with the sixth grade classes they would come back to show Woody how much they had gathered in the sheet from all of the grades.

About thirty minutes later, we heard some noise and some laughter down the hall. We all looked up in time to see Mr. Woodward, the four student body officers, and the principal trying to drag a sheet full of pennies and nickels through our doorway. There was no way that they could lift the sheet. It was too full.

We all clapped and cheered, and Woody raised his fist in the air and shouted, "All right!"

They dragged the sheet back through the door and said they would count the money that night and let us know Tuesday morning how much had been gathered on Monday.

Tuesday, the same student body officers came to our classroom. They said they had stayed with Mr. Woodward and the principal until nine o'clock the night before rolling the pennies and nickels and counting them. They wanted to know if any of us had mothers who would be willing to help count the money every night after school.

They said we wouldn't believe how much money had been gathered. We knew it would be a lot, but when they said that they had counted $513.42 the night before, we went crazy. (We weren't crazy, though, for very long. Mrs. Barker was still Mrs. Barker.)

We threw our dimes into the sheet. The student

body officers continued through the classrooms and ended up in our classroom again after their rounds.

Again, the sheet was heavy. And it was heavy on Wednesday. It wasn't so heavy on Thursday, but instead of only change, there were lots of dollar bills. I saw one-dollar bills, a twenty, some fives, and some checks. We couldn't wait until the next Monday to see how much money had been thrown into the sheet in all.

The next Sunday the missionaries came to our house again. They said that they had a surprise for us. Woody and his mom were going to get baptized!

I had no idea that someone who wasn't eight years old could get baptized. I guess I really did, but I'd always thought of someone my size getting baptized. Woody's mom was big.

The missionaries said Bishop Lee was going to baptize both Woody and his mother. He had been the one to give Woody a blessing at the hospital. They said Mrs. Blackendorf had felt something special while the bishop was giving the blessing. The missionaries had given her a Book of Mormon the week before the accident, but she hadn't even started to read it. That night, when she got home from the hospital, she started to read the Book of Mormon. She couldn't stop reading, and when she finished it she prayed about it and knew it was true.

Woody and his mom would be baptized the Saturday after Woody had his cast removed.

Monday, the assembly to give Mrs. Blackendorf and Woody the money that had been thrown onto the sheet was going to begin at two.

At one-fifty the fire alarm sounded. Mrs. Barker grabbed her roll book, hit the button on her stopwatch, and turned off the lights as we headed out of our door. We have a place on the lower playground where we line up in *A-B-C* order. It's mostly black-top and is away from the building.

It's always exciting to have a fire drill. Mrs. Barker always times us. We see how fast we can get in line. Then Mrs. Barker calls roll, and when Angela Washington (the last name on our roll) says, "Here," Mrs. Barker hits the stop button.

It was an even more exciting fire drill that day. Woody was still in his wheelchair. Jake loves competing, and beating the stopwatch at a fire drill is one of his favorite things.

While Mrs. Barker was grabbing her roll book and turning out the lights, Woody and Jake were racing to the door. Nearly everyone got out before Woody, but Jake helped bounce him down the one step outside the door, and then they were off.

I had stayed back with Julie and Mrs. Barker, so I could hear her yelling to Jake and Woody to slow down. But they couldn't hear her. They were too busy making noise of their own.

There were whoops and hollers as they went down the sloping sidewalk that led to the blacktop where we were to line up.

Jake pushed at first, then tried to keep up as the wheelchair picked up speed. Everyone cleared out of the way as the wild wheelchair went speeding down the sidewalk. Woody and Jake were shouting, "Look out below!" and "Move fast! We're coming through!" Jake finally put his feet on the posts on the back of the wheelchair and just went along for the ride.

Mrs. Barker, Julie, and I ran after them. I couldn't believe that Mrs. Barker could run so fast. We reached the bottom of the slope just about a minute after the wheelchair reached it. Jake and Woody were in their places in line acting as if nothing at all had happened.

At first I thought Mrs. Barker was going to keep both of them in for recess for a week. The look on her face would have made me beg for forgiveness. Then I was afraid she was going to have a heart attack. She was breathing hard, and she couldn't catch her breath.

She looked back and forth from Woody to Jake. They were both grinning from ear to ear. She started taking roll. And we had beaten the old record by five seconds! (Mrs. Barker had always been the last one to come to the blacktop. She had never run all the way before.)

The bell rang again to tell us to go back to class. We found out later that a sixth grader had been playing with the fire alarm. He got in so much trouble that he probably won't do that again.

But Jake and Woody didn't get in much trouble. Mrs. Barker just made them promise not to race like that again. She said Woody already had one broken leg and he didn't need the rest of his body broken.

We were ten minutes late for the assembly. But it was probably best. Mrs. Barker said that since we'd had a break our wiggles should be out of us.

Mr. Woodward spoke first. He reminded us of our assembly a few weeks before. Then he asked Mrs. Blackendorf and Woody to come to the front of the gym.

The student body president came forward, and Mr. Woodward handed him the microphone. He was carrying a huge envelope.

He said, "On behalf of all the students of East Elementary, we would like to present you with this check to be used to help pay your son's hospital bills."

Mrs. Blackendorf thanked him as she took the big envelope. They had made a huge check so that she could hold it up and show everyone. But she didn't turn it around at first. She just stared at it, and her lip started to tremble. By the time she turned it around, she was really crying. I knew that grown-ups do that sometimes when they're really happy.

The check was for $2,452.32. No wonder she was crying!

I sat there thinking about me and Elwood J. Blackendorf. I hadn't liked him. I had got mad at him. I had hated him. Then I liked him. I fasted for him. I cared about him. And I think I clapped louder than anyone else that day. We had all worked to-gether to help someone who needed help—and I was happy from the top of my head to the tips of my toes. I decided right then and there that it was worth working hard to get that kind of a feeling, because that must be how real happiness feels.

ABOUT THE AUTHOR

Bette Molgard received a bachelor's degree from Utah State University in elementary education. She has taught preschool, seminary, special education, and second-grade classes, and has worked to establish one of the first Parent Education Resource centers in the state of Utah. She is the coauthor of several activity books for children.

The author and her husband, Max H. Molgard, are the parents of six children. The family resides in Tooele, Utah.